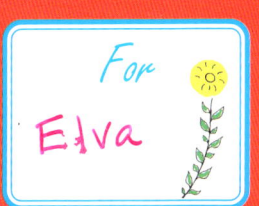

For
Elva

What's a Girl to Do?

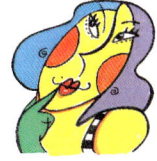

Common Sense Advice on Friendship, Romance, Work, and Self-Esteem

By Helen H. Moore
Illustrated by Paula Brinkman
Book designed by Lesley Ehlers

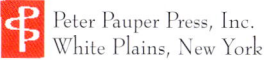

Peter Pauper Press, Inc.
White Plains, New York

*To Juno, my Godchild
(a girl who always knows
what to say and do)*

Illustrations copyright
© 1998 Paula Brinkman
Text copyright © 1998
Peter Pauper Press, Inc.
202 Mamaroneck Avenue
White Plains, NY 10601
All rights reserved
ISBN 0-88088-093-7
Printed in China
7 6 5 4 3 2 1

Contents

Introduction 4
On Friendship 6
Romance and Dating 22
At the Work Place 34
On Self-Esteem 53

Introduction

I wish I had a nickel for every time I've said to myself, while picking myself up and brushing off the debris of some *faux pas*, *gaffe*, or plain old blunder: "I wish someone had told me about that!" (I'd have a great collection of nickels!)

Oh, sure, my mother, older friends, schoolteachers, and aunts told me all kinds of things that I *shouldn't* do . . . but no one ever thought to really tell me what *to* do . . . about dating, jobs, friendships—you name it.

As a result, I've suffered through the Jobs, Dates, and Friends You-

Wouldn't-Wish-On Your-Worst-Enemy blues, until I finally figured out a few basic guidelines, some of which are offered here.

I hope they'll help you to figure out for yourself "what's a girl *to* do" as you sail through your social life, career, and relationships, especially now that we "girls" are free to dream and do anything!

H.H.M.

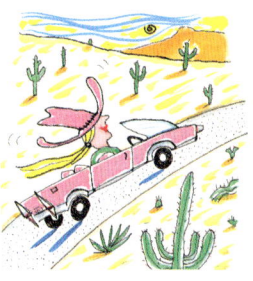

On Friendship

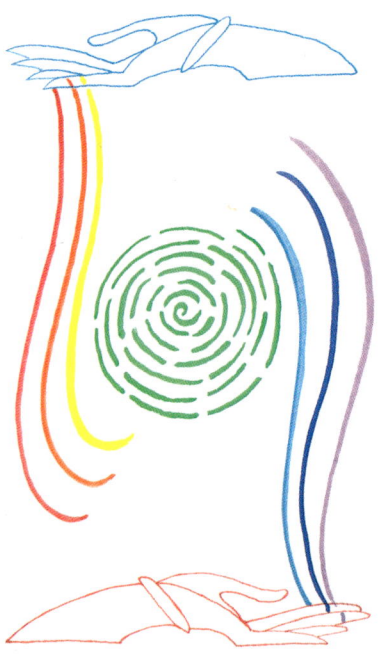

So what will a best friend tell you? That "you can do it," that she believes in you, that it's those darned pants that are making you look fat (not that you are). As my mother used to say, "A friend may be many things, but a critic isn't one of them."

What Mother told you really is true: The best way to make friends is to be friendly. This is true whether you are 16 or 60, single or married, shy or outgoing. Be friendly and others will befriend you.

Q. My best friend (I'll call her Eugenie) borrows my clothing and forgets to return it. She has also borrowed money, which she has not paid back. Whenever I go to a cultural or social event, I always invite her, but she never reciprocates. I found out—after the party!—that she had invited all her other friends. What's wrong with me?

A. The only thing wrong with you is that you have confused the words "friend" and "user." You, it seems, are one, Eugenie is the other. (And if she's your idea of a "best friend," I'd hate to meet your worst enemy!) Gather up your courage, ask for the return of your money and your clothes, and tell Eugenie that when she doesn't invite you to events/return what she's borrowed, etc., you feel hurt. Friendship is supposed to be a two-way street. If Eugenie can't or won't accept this, then you need to learn how to "just say no." (And while you're at it, maybe you should find a new best friend!)

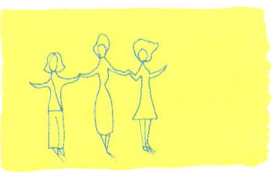

Best Activities for Making Friends

- Country and western line dancing
- Joining a charity as a volunteer
- Getting involved with amateur theatricals
- Dog walking (especially if your neighborhood has a special park or part of a park set aside for dogs and their people)
- Extra-curricular activities: adult education, art classes, chess club (maybe not)
- House of worship: Many have social activities or services for people of varying age groups.

- Pen-pal organizations. Yes, you can find them in the yellow pages, or try on-line Internet pals. But never divulge your address or agree to meet with someone you've encountered long-distance unless you take common sense precautions—like meeting in a public place, or having a trusted friend come along.

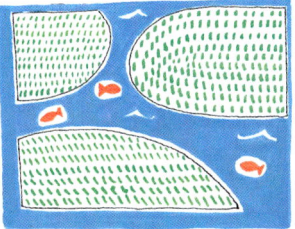

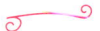

Just about every major religion or philosophy has its own version of what we in the West call "the Golden Rule:" basically, treat others as *you* would like to be treated!

In addition to being a good philosophy for life, it's an excellent rule to follow in all relationships, from casual acquaintanceships to marriage. So, "Do unto others. . ." and see the results.

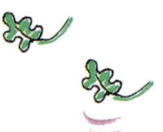

Q. I have a good friend who enjoys acting in "little theater" productions. Some of the performances have been quite enjoyable, and others just awful. I always attend anything she's in, because we're friends and I want to show support. Sometimes I can quite honestly say "That was great," or, "You were terrific." But other performances are so bad, my friend must know it. What do I say on such occasions to spare her feelings without lying?

A. Follow "the Golden Rule" and you can't go wrong. Try this approach suggested by a friend of mine (who also happens to be an amateur actor): "It was great seeing you up there." Without lying about how good the performance was, it says something kind and honest, as well (it *is* great to see a friend, isn't it?).

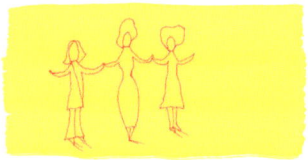

Overheard on a New York Subway:

First woman: "You've heard of people who are 'painfully shy'"?
Second woman: "Uh-huh."
First woman: "Well, she's 'painfully outgoing.'"

We've all had the experience, at a party or other social gathering, of wincing as someone dominates the conversation to the point of silencing everyone else. These poor souls—the "painfully outgoing"—don't seem to realize that the silence that greets their remarks is not an invitation to continue, but a wish that they'd stop! The best rule to follow when in any social gathering is really just what we learned in kindergarten: "Take turns." (And, as the wit said, it really can be better to keep one's mouth shut and be thought a fool, than to open one's mouth and confirm it.)

Q. I'm lucky enough to have a group of good friends, all young women like myself. Our problem? One of our group, Christina, is a non-stop motormouth! She's not mean or gossipy, she just doesn't let anyone else get a word in edgewise when we're together! How can we get her to change?

A. You can't change other people. You can, however, change the way you react to them. This Christina must take a breath sometime. Next time she does, be ready to jump in with something pithy, like "That happened to me once," or, "Oh, that reminds me . . ."

Sometimes the subtle approach doesn't work. Depending on the degree of friendship you feel, you may have to speak privately with Christina (don't gang up on her!) and in a non-threatening way explain that you love her and her interesting stories, but you feel shut out when she does so much of the talking. She probably won't like hearing it, but if she takes your words to heart, you'll have done her a favor!

Q. Tonight I came home practically in tears, and not just for the first time! A co-worker, whom I care for, who can be quite kind and thoughtful, and whom I think of as a friend, has hurt my feelings for the umpteenth time. I've known Mary for years, and she often makes a hurtful remark. Then, when she sees the look on my face, she says, "Oh, you know

I'm only joking!"

Maybe she's right, and I *am* too sensitive. But it really bugs me! What can I do to make her see what her teasing does to me?

A. If, as you say, she knows from your facial expression that she has hurt you, you're on the right track. Now pull that train into the station and speak up! Tell her, "Mary, when you say (whatever it is that bugs you), I feel hurt." That gives her the opportunity, and perhaps the impetus, to clean up her act.

I once had an acquaintance whose company I enjoyed very much. We attended the same college, enjoyed the same movies, music, and books, and laughed together till our make-up ran. She was, I thought, a real friend—a real soul mate—until the first time a guy asked her out on an evening when she and I had planned to go shopping together. She left me waiting at the local mall without so much as a phone call to cancel! Subsequently, she apologized for not having thought to call me, but then I noticed that whenever a guy would call, she'd ditch me.

I really felt hurt at first, but

afterward I was glad I found out that she put men before friends. I think a girl should be loyal to her girlfriends. And it's good manners to keep the first appointment you make no matter what temptation comes up later.

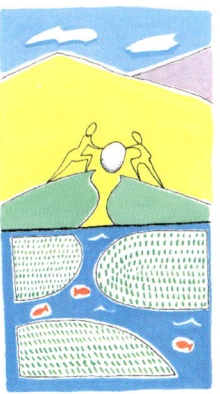

Romance and Dating

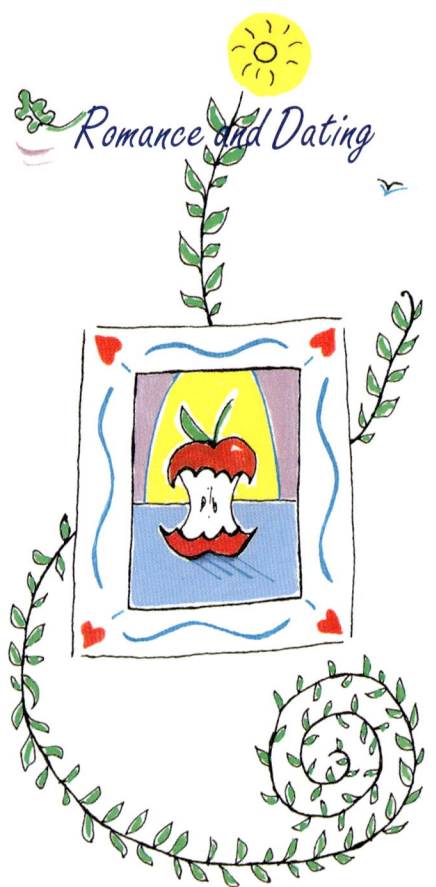

Mankind's first official attempt at dating took place in the Garden of Eden, and, like most dates, it was based on a profound misunderstanding.

Linda Sunshine,
Women Who Date Too Much
(And Those Who Should Be So Lucky)

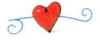

Perhaps the most important thing in any relationship is keeping the lines of communication open.

Merle Shain,
Some Men Are More Perfect than Others

Q. Every time we plan to go to a movie, my boyfriend insists on picking what we see, and it's usually a film with aliens getting blown up, or terrorists getting blown up, or bank robbers getting blown up—you get the idea. I'm about ready to blow up, myself! I prefer a romance or a mystery, but he calls those "chick flicks," and refuses to go. Are all guys like this? What can I do about it?

A. All guys, thank goodness, are not like your boyfriend, although, in truth, many do prefer an action/adventure film to a luscious romance. But where's the compromise that should be a part of any relationship? If your boyfriend won't agree to see a movie of your choice once in a while, you may want to rethink your relationship with this character.

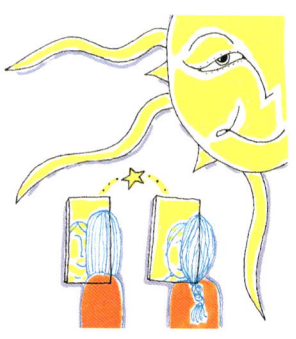

At any age, the elements of a great date have very little to do with superficial things like money, clothing, or cars, but include:

● Self-esteem: the ability to express not only what one wants, but what one doesn't want, with the expectation that one's wishes will be respected.

● Mutual Respect: agreeing on activities, neither getting one's own way nor giving in to one's partner all the time.

● A Sense of Humor: accepting one's own and one's partner's limitations (and being able to laugh about them).

● A Willingness to Take Reasonable Risks: doing something new, even if you're not sure you'll be good at it. Whether it's clog dancing or roller skating, willingness to make an attempt to enjoy oneself can lead to a whole new world of fun. (And even if it doesn't, what have you lost?)

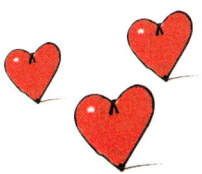

Communication is the key to a good relationship. But it's not always easy, especially since the genders have such different ways of communicating. Women like to talk about feelings: e.g., "I love walking in the rain, don't you?" Men like to talk about facts (when you can get them to talk at all!), which may explain why they like to spout statistics all the time—e.g., "Tyson bit Holyfield's left ear in the third round!" Not only that, but in the first flush of a relationship, we can both be guilty of putting our best feet forward to the extent of phoniness.

When He Says... He Really Means

When he says:
"I don't usually like cats, but I l-o-o-v-e yours!"

He really means:
"I hate cats with the white-hot intensity of a thousand suns—and that includes your little pal, Mr. Fluffy!"

When he says:
"I'm not really into sports that much."

He really means:
"I've never missed a season opener in my entire life, and I'm not about to start now."

When he says:
"Excuse the mess. My cleaning lady called in sick this week!"

He really means:
"I was hoping you'd feel like pitching in and giving me a hand!"

When he says:
"I consider myself a feminist."

He really means:
". . . ever since I found out it's a good way to get a girl to pay for dinner."

When he says:
"I'd love to go to the ballet/symphony/poetry reading!"

He really means:
". . . as much as I'd enjoy root canal without anesthesia!"

When he says:
"It's not you, it's me."
He really means:
"It's not me, it's you."

Many men dread the words, "We need to talk." How to help them get over this aversion? One great aid to communication is the "I" statement. That's a statement that allows you to tell your partner what's bothering you without blaming him. It can allow the listener to hear without becoming defensive. It's the difference between telling a person how you feel, and calling him names.

Non-"I"-Statement Communication:

She: "You're always looking at other women when we're out together!"

He: "So what?"

She: "So you're an insensitive jerk."

He: "You're just jealous . . . trying to control me . . ." etc., etc.

"I" Statement Communication:

She: "When we're together and you look at other women, I feel inadequate/hurt/jealous/." (You get the idea.)

He: "I didn't realize it bothered you."

To use "I" statements effectively, you must be aware of your own feelings, and be willing to disclose those feelings to your partner. This is the true basis of intimacy—which is, in turn, the goal of a real relationship.

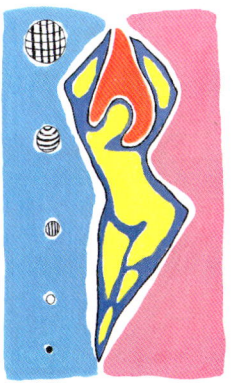

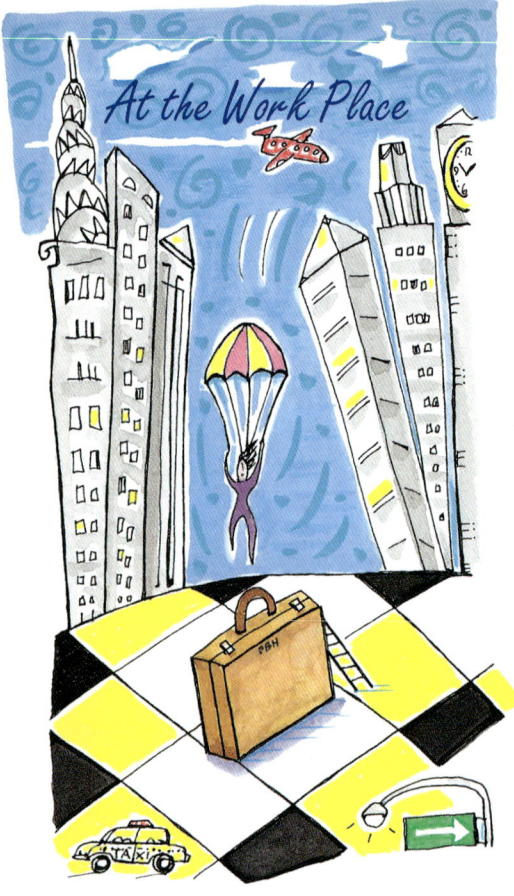

The support of other women has always been important to me, and every woman I've ever worked for has enriched my life in ways I couldn't begin to count. Nurturing, mentoring, mothering, whatever you want to call it, my woman bosses—Martha, Pat, and Terry—did a great job by challenging me to grow, as a worker and as a person, and then standing back and letting me do it. I will always be indebted to each of them. Working for a woman can be one of the greatest experiences, not just in a career, but in life itself.

Q. I've heard lots of people talking about having a "mentor" at work. Is a mentor just an older employee who "knows the ropes?" Or is there more to it than that?

A. There's a difference between a mentor and a longtime employee who just likes telling newer employees that it's their turn to clean the coffee maker.

A mentor, ideally, should hold a position higher than yours. She, therefore, has first-hand knowledge of how to succeed in the company you both work for. She can warn you what not to say to the CEO, for example, or what to wear to the corporate retreat, helping you appear more seasoned and polished than other new employees. She can recommend journals to read, trends to follow, how to dress for success in your particular company, or if dress is even an issue, and more. So seek out an older, wiser, successful employee willing to take you under her wing, and get ready to succeed.

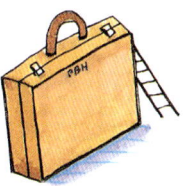

"Corporate Communications" specialists are experts at camouflaging reality with a layer of euphemism. Their most notable accomplishment was probably the introduction of the fuzzy term "downsizing" to replace the all-too-hard-edged "layoffs." (You've got to admire them: when the general public caught on, they replaced "downsizing" with "rightsizing.") Is there no end? Probably not. The only defense is preparedness. Here's a Top Ten list of corporate euphemisms, and their real meanings:

When Management Says... It Really Means

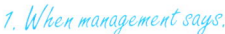

1. When management says:
"We're looking for Team Players."
It really means:
"You know, people who won't rock the boat. We don't want any potential whistleblowers!"

2. When management says:
"It's being re-evaluated."
It really means:
"We got rid of it."

3. When management says:
"This reorganization will maximize utilization of our resources."

It really means:
"Your job is toast."

4. When management says:
"We're re-engineering."
It really means:
anything from "painting the restroom," to "changing our logo" to "moving half our operations to Mexico."

5. When management says:
"Vision Statement" (sometimes called "Mission Statement" and interchangeable with "Credo")
It really means:
a meaningless hash of upbeat slogans and vague, unattainable goals,

sprinkled with words like "integrity," "facilitate," and "quality."

6. When management says:
"We consider you an exempt employee."
It really means:
"and we therefore consider ourselves exempt from having to pay you overtime." (You don't mind working those 60-hour weeks, do you?)

7. When management says:
"The Company is undergoing a Paradigm Shift."
It really means:
"We're in the midst of the frantic mid-course correction that ensues

when management finally realizes the company is radically out-of-step with the rest of the industry."

8. When management says:
"We're restructuring."
It really means:
same as #3.

9. When management says:
"Come on, get out of your 'Comfort Zone!'"
It really means:
"Here, take on these additional tasks left undone by the workers who were 'reorganized' during the Paradigm Shift (or was it the Restructuring?)."

10. When management says:

"There's a light at the end of the tunnel."

It really means:

"Unfortunately, it's the oncoming train known as Chapter 11."

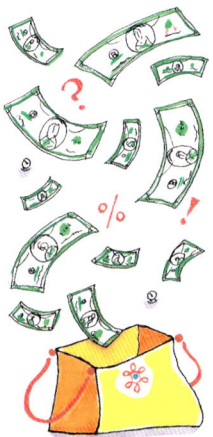

Q. My boss just informed me I'll be representing the company at a big conference in a month. Although I've traveled a lot, this will be my first business trip, and I'm a little nervous. Is traveling for business so different from traveling for pleasure? What are the *do's* and *don'ts*?

A. Traveling on business can be fun, and a great way to see parts of the world you might not ordinarily go to on vacation—like Detroit. Here's a helpful list of some things to do (and not do) when traveling on business.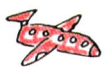

Do: Check with your boss to see if you can take a vacation day on your return before coming back into the office.
Don't: Take the red-eye back (from anywhere) so you can be in the office the same day you return. Trust me, your heading straight to the office from the airport won't do you or your firm any good.

Do: Label separate envelopes "Meals," "Carfare," "Miscellaneous," etc., keep them in your bag, and file receipts as you get them. Jot a key word on the back of each, explaining what it's for. This makes it a lot easier to complete your expense report.

Don't: Stuff receipts into your wallet, bag, or pocketbook. Another tip—accounting departments tend to look askance at receipts written on crumpled-up cocktail napkins.

Do: Invite clients to lunch and dinner. It's a legitimate expense, and one reason companies encourage employee attendance at distant conferences.

Don't: Sit on your bed eating room service meals and watching in-room movies. It's hard to convince your boss that eating shrimp cocktail, filet mignon, and chocolate mousse, and watching *Cabana Boys in Trouble* ten times is a legitimate entertainment expense.

Do: Bring a journal to keep notes on all meetings, workshops, speeches or seminars you attend, so you can write a top-notch report on your return.

Don't: Trust your memory. Your report will be so thin, your boss will suspect you spent the whole conference at the hotel's Karaoke bar with the staff from the local office.

Do: Take carry-on luggage only. You can't afford to spend three days of a four-day trip waiting for your luggage to be rerouted from Kuala Lumpur, or wherever the airline might send it.

Don't: Take too much clothing. Separates you can mix and match are best, with one fairly dressy outfit for any dinners or mixers that are scheduled. And leave the glamorous high-heels at home, especially if you'll be attending a trade show. Convention center floors are brutal on your feet!

[A woman] is not needed to think man's thoughts . . . Hers is not to preserve the man-made world, but to create a human world by the infusion of the feminine element into all of its activities.

Margaret Sanger

When we first started entering the "male-dominated" workforce, too many of us women were made to feel that we had to act, think, and dress like men in order to succeed.

All of those female executives of the early '80s in their blue suits with little "feminine" bow ties had to try so hard because they had few female role models to emulate!

How terrific it is that now a woman at work *can* succeed while wearing feminine clothes if she chooses. She can empathize with, and show caring toward, her staff if she is a manager, and admit to using intuition in making decisions. In short, a woman today can succeed in the workplace, not by imitating a man, but by being a woman!

Q. Now that I've just been promoted to "team leader," I'm struggling with how to act toward people who used to be my co-workers, and are now my subordinates. Should I detach myself from them, and perhaps even be considered a bit cold? A lot of them are women whose lives I've shared for several years, through ups and downs, laughter and tears. Now I have to supervise them but I don't really want to "boss" them around. Help!

A. Did you ever have one of those teachers who was a real friend, sharing feelings, and even joking with students, but also able to command respect and "get the job done?" You can do the same. By all means keep an empathetic ear open to your staff and co-workers, and treat them like human beings, but show by example that there's a time for socializing, and a time for work.

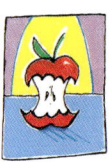

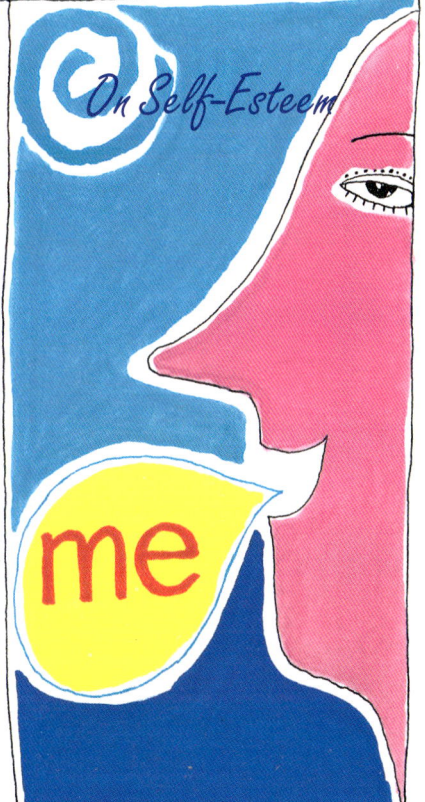

There's a lot of talk about self-esteem these days. It seems pretty basic to me. If you want to feel proud of yourself, you've got to do things you can be proud of.

Osceola McCarty,
Washerwoman-turned-philanthropist

Self-esteem. What is it? Not overbearing pride, or conceit, but a feeling of well-being in one's own skin. How do you know you have it? Try this quiz:

Answer each of the following questions with one of these answers:

Yes, most of the time
Maybe
Once in a while
I suppose
Who, me?
No way!

Are you content with yourself?
Can you absorb occasional criticisms or hurts without going into an emotional tailspin?
Are you able to compromise, letting others have their own way sometimes?
Is it okay with you if you're not always the center of attention?

If you checked, "Yes, most of the time," to most of these questions, then your self-esteem is probably okay.

Q. I like to shop at thrift and vintage clothing stores and put together my own "look," and lots of people compliment me. But one friend, Arielle, needles me. She wears only designer labels and the latest styles. When people compliment me, Arielle says, "Oh, I could never wear anything second-hand," or "You should only buy designer labels; that way you know you're getting the best!" I have to admit that Arielle's criticism gets on my nerves. How can I get her to stop?

A. You might try taking her to lunch and telling her (in a nice way) that her remarks bother you. Arielle's comments sound as if they spring from low self-esteem. Maybe she doesn't think her own taste is good enough, so she needs a designer label on her clothing for reassurance, like a "seal of approval." Let her know that you feel confident in your taste, and that being your own designer leaves you money to spend on other things—like taking friends to lunch!

The better we feel about ourselves, the fewer times that we have to knock somebody else down to feel tall.

Odetta

Lacking self-esteem, people of all ages are vulnerable to anyone or anything that promises to make them feel special or important—and too often, those things are potentially harmful. But the good news is that low self-esteem doesn't have to be a permanent condition.

If you recognize that your self-esteem is a little low, you can build it up. Start by taking stock of your achievements (even if they're not earth-shattering, but simply ordinary things, like getting up in the morning and 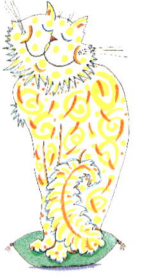 doing your best at school or work, or some special hobby or skill that you are striving to perfect). Building on that basis, try to do other things you can feel good about.

And if there are things about yourself that are causing you to feel less than worthwhile, change them. Start small if you have to. And remember that you are special and precious, and you can do it!

Q. A friend of mine is into reading self-help books and says I should try giving myself "positive affirmations." Just what are "positive affirmations," and how do they work?

A. "Positive affirmations" is a technique people sometimes use to boost their self-esteem. These are just positive thoughts you "tell" yourself repeatedly, on the theory that, with repetition, positive thinking will become second nature.

Here are some samples:

1. Rather than saying, "I'm not going to eat fattening foods" (negative), say "I'm going to treat my body to a healthy diet" (positive).

2. A direct, short sentence like "I can succeed at my diet," may be all it takes.

3. When you eat a delicious, low-fat fruit salad, for example, you can repeat, "I enjoy treating my body to wholesome foods!"

The more frequently you repeat these affirmations, the sooner you'll believe them, and, the theory goes, they will become reality.

Try it—you'll like it—and you may like yourself more, too!

Q. I grew up in a small college town, where I was always a "leader"—in scouting, in school, and among my friends. I put myself through our local college on a scholarship, worked summers as an intern in my chosen field, and, now that graduation is approaching, I've got a job offer from a prestigious firm in a big city. My problem? As graduation nears, I'm getting more and more anxious about my future. Do you think this is because I have low self-esteem?

A. It's unlikely that someone of your accomplishments suffers from a lack of self-esteem. What you're describing sounds more like a lack of confidence. There's a difference. We can have a healthy sense of self-esteem, but lack the confidence to try something for the first time. Call on the inner strength that has always made you a leader, and forge ahead. Once you have a few successes at your new job, your self-confidence will probably return.

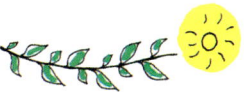

Sometimes people (friends included) take some degree of pleasure in another's distress. It's what Oscar Wilde must have felt when he admitted, "It's not enough that I should succeed—my friends must fail!" We've all had acquaintances and friends who admire and love us when we're successful, but love us even more when we're failing—because that helps them feel better about themselves. There is one sure way to handle such friends: Make sure that you are your own friend first, and then make some new ones too. You'll know that your self-esteem is at a high level when you surround yourself with people who are confident enough to applaud *your* achievements.